First World War
and Army of Occupation
War Diary
France, Belgium and Germany

1 DIVISION
Divisional Troops
76 Field Company Royal Engineers
1 April 1919 - 31 August 1919

WO95/1254/3

The Naval & Military Press Ltd
www.nmarchive.com
Published in association with The National Archives

Published by

The Naval & Military Press Ltd

Unit 10 Ridgewood Industrial Park,

Uckfield, East Sussex,

TN22 5QE England

Tel: +44 (0) 1825 749494

www.naval-military-press.com

www.nmarchive.com

This diary has been reprinted in facsimile from the original. Any imperfections are inevitably reproduced and the quality may fall short of modern type and cartographic standards.

© **Crown Copyright**
Images reproduced by permission of The National Archives, London, England, 2015.

Contents

Document type	Place/Title	Date From	Date To
Heading	WO95/1254/3		
Heading	B E F 1 Div Troops (Western Div) 76 Fld Coy RE.s Previously with Gds Div 1919 Apr to 1919 Aug		
Heading	76th Field Coy. R.E. for the month of April-1919		
War Diary	Merten.	01/04/1919	30/04/1919
Heading	War Diary Original of the 76th Field Coy R.E. for the month of May. 1919		
War Diary	Merten Germany.	01/05/1919	30/06/1919
Heading	Original War Diary of the 76th Field Company. R E. for the month of July-1919		
War Diary	Merten Germany.	21/07/1919	31/07/1919
Heading	Original War Diary of the 76th Field Company R.E. for the month of August-1919		
War Diary	Merten Germany.	01/08/1919	23/08/1919
War Diary	Troop Train	24/08/1919	25/08/1919
Heading	Headquarters Kinmel Park Camp		
Heading	Original War Diary of the 78th Field Co. R E to complete the month of August 1919		
War Diary	Kinmel Park Camp	26/08/1919	31/08/1919

WO95/1234/3

BEF

1 Div Troops
(Western Div)

76 Fld Coy R.E.s
Previously with Gds Div

1919 APR to 1919 AUG

CONFIDENTIAL

ORIGINAL

WAR DIARY
of the
76th Field Coy. R.E.
for the month of
APRIL - 1919

Army Form C. 2118.

WAR DIARY
or
INTELLIGENCE SUMMARY.
(Erase heading not required.)

16th Field C.R.E. WESTERN DIVISION

Page 1.

Instructions regarding War Diaries and Intelligence Summaries are contained in F.S. Regs., Part II. and the Staff Manual respectively. Title pages will be prepared in manuscript.

Place	Date	Hour	Summary of Events and Information	Remarks and references to Appendices
MERTEN	1.4.19		The Company is engaged in settling down. Most of the houses are under cover in large building belonging to a firm/grower. Most are in similar stables scattered through the village. What trade superior gave men billeted in houses among the civil population. Section has set up at Rent. Beautiful houses engaged in building huts for General Wittwald. No 3 Section under 2nd Lieut. Ace Johnny erecting latrines, cookhouses incinerators etc at Wittwaldhave.	
do.	2.4.19		3 O.R. Sevoltings. No 1 & 2 Sections who have supplied men to No 3 other two sections split up to start and are at work in Commerce for enlarged workshop Cart Ronce Rues for lamps etc for Rueneal Wittwaldhof. Enlarging No. 8.6. Wittwaldhof. Clearing garage, wooden building to look after horses. Nos 3 & 4 Sections working on it. afternoon.	
do.	3.4.19		2. O.R. Sevoltings. Traffic in canal to be cut. Ambulance at present in Turgan, Turgan to Salvage at Ruragen Panne ins. 13 O.R. paid to Canyon. No 468 N.V.Co Rg.	
do.	4.4.19		2 O.R. Sevoltings. Unit carried on as in 3rd. No 3 starts a cookhouse & Coy'a Hedqrs at DUISDORF & also barn into garage etc.	
do.	5.4.19		3 O.R. Sevoltings. Unit carried on as for 3rd. Clearing stanchions waggons, all demolished men employed been brought here to do own Section or Detachment.	

WAR DIARY
or
INTELLIGENCE SUMMARY. 76th Field Co. R.E. Page 2

WESTERN DIVISION

Army Form C. 2118.

Place	Date	Hour	Summary of Events and Information	Remarks and references to Appendices
MERTEN.	6.4.19		Sunday – A Reinforcement Picture at 10.30 hrs to Lecture parties of other ranks disbanded. – 3 O.R. transferred 2 Sergts + 58 O.R. posted to Company from 467 Field Co. R.E.	
do.	7.4.19		Work as usual carried out. No 3 Section start party working at AFTER improving cooking arrangements, latrines etc. 2 Lieut. R.C.P. JAMES, reports for duty on posting from 203rd Field Co. R.E.	
do.	8.4.19		Work carried on as on 7th. Cleaning up general, issues etc. at MERTEN. Lieut. F.G. DICKINSON. M.C. transferred to 137 Army Troops Co. R.E. having been with the Company since October 1916.	
do.	9.4.19		3 O.R. Demobilized. Orders to AFTER were to send 2nd Bdge. who prepared and meant to keep two sections working in a forward area. This involves enemy lines, front etc in order of priority, — damage to first estate in Chateau where are a B Row ch etc — water carriage, went there, Others incinerators, delousing huts, cookhouses etc. A Section working two were detailed to Withastielet namely I.G.R. from Comby from 428 Coy R.E. Jr. ROSSFIELD returning to Company. Demobilizations --	
do.	10.4.19		Work on Progress on 7th. No 3 Section started work with AFTER at Chateau, incinerators etc.	
do.	11.4.19		C.S.M. Carter + 4 O.R. Demobilized. Work as on 10th. Work started on Company Cookhouse and drying room etc.	

Army Form C. 2118.

WAR DIARY
INTELLIGENCE SUMMARY.

(Erase heading not required.)

76th Field Coy. R.E. — Page 3.
WESTERN DIVISION

Place	Date	Hour	Summary of Events and Information	Remarks and references to Appendices
MERTEN	12.4.19		4 O.R. Demobilized. 2 O.R. (ou. Coy on transfer from 153rd Field Coy R.E. after a lecture to (U.P.E.) by Lt. Stringfellow M.C. and Royal Engineers. The Band of the Militia and Natives of the Centre of Germany. The performance thoroughly appreciated. Roll onwards as on 10th except those were also marked Letter the Coy. 2 O.R. on Leave Home from MECKENHEIM to WITTERSCHLICK.	
do	13.4.19		2 O.R. Demobilized. Sergt J.C. BOUSFIELD, M.C. Leave Coy to Demobilization Field Gen'd H.Q.G. in 1914. Commisioned R.T.C. in Feb 1916. Platoon must. Prisoner in March 1916 + escapes from captivity from a tunnel in hut letters from German camp at CREFELD. No. 21512. May. Church Parade at 11.00 A.M.	
do	14.4.19		Work as on 10th. Cooking lunch at Duesdorf stated Pulham hut repaired from small huts. So far erected in Rawnsley Witterschlick and another (Twelve Huts) in front of 100 strong Hun prisoners. Have kept ..... ostensibly or otherwise but in charge Lt. Taegee. Capt. S. FOSTER M.C. returned to 26th G.R.E. from Coblenz home.	
do	15.4.19		Work as on 14th	
do	16.4.19		Sgts Cairn + Gleave and 8 O.R. Return to Demobilization .... carried on as on 14th.	

Army Form C. 2118.

WAR DIARY
or
INTELLIGENCE SUMMARY.

(Erase heading not required.)

76th Field Co. R.E.
WESTERN DIVISION.
Page 4

Place	Date	Hour	Summary of Events and Information	Remarks and references to Appendices
MERTEN.	17.4.19.		Junior Staff Sergt. Kirkham, Sergt Sterne, M.M. and Cpl. Underwood + 8 O.R. sent away for Demobilization today — L/Cpl Cavish on leave on 19th	
do	18.4.19		GOOD FRIDAY. General Holiday. Voluntary Service at 11.30 hrs - 10 O.R. demobilized today — 4 2.0.R. Posted. 5. N.C.O. from 153rd Field Co. + Capt A.L. Colville from Canton ne Section Commanders in exchange from 204 Field Co. R.E. and Capt. J. G. Foster.	
do	19.4.19.		8 O.R. demobilized today + 4 O.R. on Co. from 463rd Field Co. R.E. Reconstruction unknown Wilhelm. Seal. Concrete Performance + declared unsafe etc. had cinema-trip to blow-up. Work carried on as on 18.4.19. Asst. 400yd Hung front Revert tint started erection wooden platform in lieu of WITTERSHEIM.	
do	20.4.19		EASTER DAY — Service at 11.30 hrs — L.C.P.E. 3. O.R. Demobilized.	
do	21.4.19.		Work on on 19th. Butts and outside started at MACKENHEIM. 2 no 3 Lect. Guns ditch at ALFTER Mixed, also work in connection Delomer Station Refugee Machine.	
do	22.4.19		Work as 21st	
do	23.4.19		Work as 21st 1.O.R. Demobilized today.	
do	24.4.19		Work as 21st 2 O.R. having volunteered for Service in Russia are sent to CHATHAM today.	
do	25.4.19		CO. + L/S. Tidswell + 1 N.C.O. to CHATHAM to Serve in Russia. Will carry to on 21st. 400yd platform for putting total overdue wider ripped away. else have been erected. Trestles for	

(A8004) D.D. & L., London, E.C.
Wt. W1771/Mar 31 750,000 5/17 Sch. 52 Forms/C2118/14

Army Form C. 2118.

Page 5.

WAR DIARY
of
INTELLIGENCE SUMMARY. 16th Field C.R.E.
WESTERN DIVISION.

(Erase heading not required.)

Instructions regarding War Diaries and Intelligence Summaries are contained in F. S. Regs., Part II. and the Staff Manual respectively. Title pages will be prepared in manuscript.

Place	Date	Hour	Summary of Events and Information	Remarks and references to Appendices
MERTEN	25.4.19.		Our complete new slip infantry in the hands of the 1st line troops. Lieut W. REID M.C. joins Coy from 55th Field C.R.E.	
do	26.4.19.		Intd. on 21st A continuation of post duties. Lieut Col VOLMERSHOVEN, by his Action. 1 O.R. joins Unit from 55 Field C.R.E. No Return of refugees at night to Patrol VITTERSHICK. On urgent orders from 2nd Bde. The Majority of the Section returned to & entered the Bridgehead within an hour of notice. Peaceful night. 2 O.R. Demobilised.	
do	27.4.19		2. O.R. Demobilised. SUNDAY. Intoxicated Civil Police at 11.00 p.m.	
do	28.4.19.		Intd. on 26th. A Court was held at MERTEN. Scoup in confidence in use notifying but also drunkenness made. At R.E.s disposal for one hour.	
do	29.4.19		Intd. on 26th. For charge whether has been setting are sober & well.	
do	30.4.19		Intd. on 26th. Running on the 1 Sapper C. Sm. Formann Staff C.S.E + 3 Sgts + 64 O.R. have been demobilised. Two men were left on last line demobilised.	
			Strength Sheet / Company.	
			Capt. J. COLVILLE, 2/Lt, Commander.	
			2/Lt. N.a. RANDALL Section No.1 Off.	
			2/Lt. S.W.J. Casgro " 2 "	
			2/Lt. A.C. Jennings " 3 "	
			2/Lt. R.C.P. James " 4 "	
			Lieut W. Reid - D.E. Staff officer.	

Merten, Germany
1.5.19

J. Colville Major R.E.
O/C 16 Field Coy R.E.

CONFIDENTIAL

WAR DIARY
ORIGINAL
of the
76th Field Coy. R.E.

for the month of
MAY. 1919.

WAR DIARY
INTELLIGENCE SUMMARY

Army Form C. 2118.

76th FIELD COMPANY R.E.
WESTERN DIVISION.

Place	Date	Hour	Summary of Events and Information	Remarks and references to Appendices
MERTEN Germany	1.5.19		No 1 Section at WITTERSCHLICK have completed work to WD. No forced labour available. Party of small party of inhabitants found also undertaking bombs etc. 1000 F.P. small arms ammunition, a few rounds of howitzer ammunition and a number latrines, and arms found. After pointing out the value of same, they were handed over again to the German railway authorities have orders to file down the triggers of same. No 2 Section have completed a workshop & lead to works & numerous other MERTEN. Inhabitants welcome workers and willingly assist as much as they are able to. Latrines & numerous outbuildings are continually being hacked in enormous walls. Has not the cafe to shelter sent to No 3 Section still at MECKENHEIM. H.Q. Co. moved into Mess. Cookhouses still at Mess. Cookhouses will be given on Monday, small men dem. from DISBOKE buildings & lattis making, three tennis courts & small etc and for sports. VENTERSHOVEN mine Co. Postal Cookhouses & others AFTER completing constructing work to Wagentrophie, section working on erection huts for section to & wagentrophie. H days	
	2.5.19		Work as carried on as in May. 15th. Leave to U.K. granted Capt. A.J. COLVILLE & 2nd Lieut. R.C.P. JAMES. Since discovering stores in MERTEN instructions will not go to work except in large parties. Int. Group found to be too indefinite	

Army Form C. 2118.

WAR DIARY
INTELLIGENCE SUMMARY.

(Erase heading not required.)

76th Field Company R.E.
WESTERN DIVISION

Place	Date	Hour	Summary of Events and Information	Remarks and references to Appendices
MERTEN Germany	3.5.19		Work carried on as on 1/5/19. Lieut C.J CREED. M.C. reported to duty transferred from 55th Field Co. R.E. Party from Company made quick trip from BONN to COBLENZ & return.	
do-	4.5.19		Sunday. Voluntary Church Parade to Englehuchel.	
do	5.5.19		Work carried on as on 1st. A site selected to Billet & Stores at ALFTER by G.O.C. 2nd Bgde - a store huts at DUSDORF also selected - Lieut W. REID M.C. takes over duties of Business Staff Officer from 2/Lt. E.W.F. CRAGGS, who returns to Adjutant Company.	
do	6.5.19		Work carried on as on 1st. Site of hut to billet MT Co. selected at BONN. 1 O.R. arrived on reinforcement from 153 Field Co. R.E.	
do	7.5.19		Work as on 1st. Remains at WITTERSHICK opened to disinfection. Arrangements made for mess of 2 Coys & 232 Cop Coy to mess at MECKENHEIM.	
do	8.5.19		Work as on 1st. 1 O.R. Pers Corps arr. on reinforcement from 236 Cp.R.E. Coy.	
do	9.5.19		Work as on 1st.	
do	10.5.19		Work as on 1st.	
do	11.5.19.		Sunday. Voluntary Church Parade.	

WAR DIARY or INTELLIGENCE SUMMARY

Army Form C. 2118.

76th Field Coy R.E.
WESTERN DIVISION

Place	Date	Hour	Summary of Events and Information	Remarks and references to Appendices
MERTEN GERMANY	12.5.19		No. 1. have completed Range at WITTERSHICK & are making overheads to range in wet weather. Return 75% completed. Munchine Range No. 2 Batts at FLIERZHEIM started - men left No. 3 to assist them. No. 3 have completed Cookhouse Orderly room at VELMEISHOVEN at ALFTER being spring cleaned & re-reserved. Battn. S/L Room C. Coy (1) 58 (Welsh) Transport lines - B Coy Cookhouses to completed. Battn rooms 70% complete. Adbrns 40%, 45% completed. MECKENHEIM 23rd & 26th Coys started unit cleaning inspection Cookhouses etc. Cookhouse in B Coy complete, Y C Coy 50%. Ablution benches & shelters complete. DUISDORF at Brigade HQ Schools & Canteens work been completed. Incinerator 80% complete. Two Searchlights built. 3 Latrines vermin in 4 one cookhouse plaster completed. ISR from Coy hq - at Table Plate Panel. 1 OR from No. 1 WT. No. 2 + 4 Porters men & amd 2/Lt MERTEN went leave. Carried on same above on 12th.	3.
do.	13.5.19		No. MERTEN & TRIPPELSDORF & 2nd June M 15th C taken over - Formalities of handing over gear waiting Sat Sup.	
do.	14.5.19		Work as on 12th. Small parts started putting roof to a very large Hut. Extensive Lecture each afternoon taking place in small fine portal steam saws being worked hourly gentagain - 1 OR from Coy hqrs S 8th Fld Coy Rg. next CREED See S Gunner Ave material work Reconnaissance -	

Army Form C. 2118.

WAR DIARY
— or —
INTELLIGENCE SUMMARY.
(Erase heading not required.)

76th Field Coy R.E.
WESTERN DIVISION

Instructions regarding War Diaries and Intelligence Summaries are contained in F. S. Regs., Part II. and the Staff Manual respectively. Title pages will be prepared in manuscript.

Place	Date	Hour	Summary of Events and Information	Remarks and references to Appendices
MERTEN - GERMANY	15.5.19		Work carried on as on 12th.	
do -	16.5.19		2/Lt. E.W.F. CRAGGS granted 14 days leave to U.K. Started 17th	
do -	17.5.19		Work as on 12th. Civilian amateur tennis out Frohnlich lawn. Interest in press - putting green in. Lieut. CREED M.C. returns from water Reconnaissance.	
do -	18.5.19		Sunday. Voluntary Church parades.	
do -	19.5.19		No. 1 Section Huts plants & Range - putting green lattice at WITTERSCHLICK. Turning on miniature range at FLERZ HEIM. No. 3 at ALFTER new Reserves 50% + Baths 70% complete. Work on Cookhouse & Oven trench to drains etc being carried on. A/Bridge etc over Paddle Room 75% completed. Recreation Room Finish - DUISDORF Radios Stove 60% complete - MECKENHEIM Batteries 50% complete. Two Cr. Cookhouses completed. Latrine made + Papelle. Room 25% complete. Ovens + wash-benches now made. Capt. A.A. COLVILLE returns from leave to U.K.	
do -	20.5.19		Work as on 19th. 4 men at ROISDORF putting up sheds at D.E. Yard.	
do	21.5.19		Work as on 19th. Test intrench almost home line completed on large dug started. Wireless Aerial when fixed up - tall bivvi Washerwomen inside attend & also returns from 14 days leave to U.K. Lieut. R.E.P. JAMES I.O.R. joins Coy from 237 Ft. Bty. Cy R.A.	

WAR DIARY
INTELLIGENCE SUMMARY

Army Form C. 2118.

76th Field Coy R.E.
WESTERN DIVISION.

Place	Date	Hour	Summary of Events and Information	Remarks and references to Appendices
MERTEN Germany	22.5.19		Work to carried on as on 19th Terms sent Flying 28:30 Coy brought to TRIPPELSDORF	5
do	23.5.19		Work as on 19th Subs horses that have transport for us will Co. from TRIPPELSDORF to BRUHL where the entrainin-	
do	24.5.19		Work as on 19th No section moves from WITTERSHLICK to DUISDORF to fit new windows to GLEVENEN	
do	25.5.19		Sunday. Voluntary Church parade in evening.	
do	26.5.19		No 1 Section erecting cook house and annex to 51st Section Batt at DUISDORF. No 3 Section at ALFTER have completed 5 tank weeks 3 Incinerators 1 Cook house. Is still continuing. Alterations to road houses. Alterations to W.C. engaged at Chateau e.c. Battle house. Done 90% complete. Staves 85%. Range completed. Annex with copper tank to Cook house. HECKENHEIM refitting WC. a concrete platform not started to built Civilian latrine	
	27.5.19		Work carried on as 26th. Teams from MERTEN to carry in wounds 26th C. R.E. cage to EUSKIRCHEN Return with ours. 4 OR Recruits 75 C R.E. joined 3 OR sent to demob for entrainment to U.K.	
do	28.5.19		Work on 26th 3 OR A.C.JENNINGS admitted to dump to U.K.	
do	29.5.19		Work as on 26th. 1 + 9 R joined Coy from 42nd Div C.E.	

Army Form C. 2118.

WAR DIARY
or
INTELLIGENCE SUMMARY.
(Erase heading not required.)

76th Field Co R.E.
WESTERN DIVISION.

Remarks and references to Appendices: 6

Place	Date	Hour	Summary of Events and Information
MERTEN Germany	30.5.19		No 1 Section move to MORENHOVEN relieving a Section of 487 Field Co R.E on work in Artillery Range Area, No 4. Section where Section (487 Field Co) at BORNHEIM will work on Bonn-St Area. No 2 Section takes over work at D.H.Q. EICK 10-2, & WESSELING Pom School, 487 Field Co R.E. No 3 Section except No 2 were complete with transport.
do.	31.5.19		Work started at BORNHEIM in replacing, Slates etc at MORENHOVEN, RAMARSHOVEN, SWIM HEIM in cookhouses, wash-houses, at D.H.Q. in water, electric, heating, hutting, slating etc - WESSELING Waken Latrines - No 3 Company on work as per 13 E.R. Route 75. 2nd Co R.E & 2 S.R. to 487 Field Co R.E. modification of strength. Strength of Officers:

2 in command. Capt. A.S. COLVILLE.
O.C. No 1 Sect. 2/Lt. N.A. BLANDFORD-NEWSON.
" No 2 " 2/Lt. E.W.F. CRASSE.
" No 3 " 2/Lt. A.C. JENNINGS.
" No 4 " Lt. R.C.P. JAMES.
Supernumerary Lt. C. I. CREED. M.C.
D.E. Store Officer. Lt. W. REID. M.C.

Merten Germany. 1.6.19.

R.E 2nd Army R.E.
O.E. 76th Field Co R.E.

Army Form C. 2118.

WAR DIARY
of
INTELLIGENCE SUMMARY.
(Erase heading not required.)

76th FIELD COY RE
WESTERN DIVISION

Instructions regarding War Diaries and Intelligence Summaries are contained in F. S. Regs., Part II. and the Staff Manual respectively. Title pages will be prepared in manuscript.

Place	Date	Hour	Summary of Events and Information	Remarks and references to Appendices
MERTEN GERMANY	1-6-19		Church parade at ROSBERG. (C of E)	
	2-6-19		No 1 Section at MORENHOVEN building cookhouses, latrines and making improvements to water supply at various villages in Divisional Artillery area. No 2 Section working at EICHOLZ SCHLOSS (Divisional H.Q.) and at WESSELING also outfitting men for Coy work on wagons, bicycles &c at MERTEN. No 3 Section at ALFTER working at baths, cookhouses, latrines &c at various villages in 2nd Western Infantry Brigade area. No 4 Section at BORNHEIM doing similar work in area of 1st Western Infantry Brigade. 1 o.r. joined Coy from 75th Field Coy RE. 3 o.r. joined Coy from 409th Field Coy RE	
	3-6-19		do	
	4-6-19		do	
	5-6-19		do Recreation in afternoon. 1 Lt. CRAGG returned from leave U.K. 1 o.r. joined Coy from R.O.D. 1 o.r. joined Coy from 90th Field Coy 1 o.r. joined Coy from 249th Field Coy RE. 1 o.r. left Coy on demob	

Army Form C. 2118.

WAR DIARY
INTELLIGENCE SUMMARY.
(Erase heading not required.)

Instructions regarding War Diaries and Intelligence Summaries are contained in F. S. Regs., Part II. and the Staff Manual respectively. Title pages will be prepared in manuscript.

76th FIELD COY RE WESTERN DIVISION

Place	Date	Hour	Summary of Events and Information	Remarks and references to Appendices
MERTEN GERMANY	6-6-19		Work as on 2nd.	
	7-6-19		do. Recreation in afternoon. 1/Lt. NEWSON proceeded on 14 days leave to UK.	
	8-6-19		No parade. MAJOR G.R. EVANS granted leave to UK. 8-6-19 to 8-7-19	
	9-6-19		General Holiday.	
	10-6-19		Work as on 2nd.	
	11-6-19		do	
	12-6-19		Recreation in afternoon	
	13-6-19		do	
			No 1 Section returned from MORENHOVEN to MERTEN. Remainder of Coy work as on 2nd.	
	14-6-19		No 1 Section work on entraining Coy. Cookhouse and horse line. Remainder of Coy work as on 2nd. 1 o.r. joined Coy from 75th Field Coy R.E. 2 o.r. left Coy on demob. Recreation in afternoon. 1/Lt JENNING returned from leave to UK.	
	15-6-19		Left BONN to COBLENZ to attend funeral parade service at ROSBERG (C. of E.) Voluntary Church Parade service on 14-6-19	
	16-6-19		do	
	17-6-19		do	
	18-6-19		Recreation in afternoon. 1/Lt. CRAGGS to hospital	

Army Form C. 2118.

WAR DIARY
INTELLIGENCE SUMMARY.
(Erase heading not required.)

Instructions regarding War Diaries and Intelligence Summaries are contained in F. S. Regs., Part II. and the Staff Manual respectively. Title pages will be prepared in manuscript.

76th FIELD COY. RE
WESTERN DIVISION

Place	Date	Hour	Summary of Events and Information	Remarks and references to Appendices
MERTEN GERMANY	19-6-19		Work as 14th	
	20-6-19		No 3 Section proceeded to BONN with 2nd Western Infantry Brigade as part of the re-distribution of troops consequent on the promulgation of the event of the peace treaty not being signed. Remainder of Coy work as on 14th. Lt Capon went on leave.	
	21-6-19		Reception in afternoon "Lt Newson signed from leave	
	22-6-19		Voluntary Church service at TRIPPLESDORF (C of E)	
	23-6-19		Work as on 14th.	
	24-6-19		do	
	25-6-19		do Reception in afternoon 2 drivers transferred 575th Coy RE	
	26-6-19		I.O.R. proceeded on demob. work as on 14th. 2 or to hospital	
	27-6-19		do	
	28-6-19		do Reception in afternoon	
	29-6-19		No parades.	

Army Form C. 2118.

WAR DIARY
INTELLIGENCE SUMMARY.
(Erase heading not required.)

76th FIELD COY RE
WESTERN DIVISION

Place	Date	Hour	Summary of Events and Information	Remarks and references to Appendices
MERTEN GERMANY.	30-6-19		Work as 14.8.	
			Officers on Coy strength at end of month	
			MAJOR G. R. EVANS M.C. on leave to U.K.	
			CAPT. A. J. COLVILLE	
			LIEUT. C. J. CREED M.C.	
			" W. REID M.C. D.E. Stores Officer	
			" R.C.P. JAMES	
			2ND " E.W.F. CRAGGS in hospital	
			" " A.C. JENNINGS	
			" " N.A.B. NEWSON	

A. J. Colville Capt RE
O/C 76th Field Coy RE

CONFIDENTIAL

ORIGINAL
WAR DIARY
of the
76th Field Company, R.E.
for the month of
JULY. 1919.

Army Form C. 2118.

WAR DIARY
or
INTELLIGENCE SUMMARY.   76th Field Coy. R.E.
Western Division - Sheet 3

(Erase heading not required.)

Instructions regarding War Diaries and Intelligence Summaries are contained in F. S. Regs., Part II. and the Staff Manual respectively. Title pages will be prepared in manuscript.

Place	Date	Hour	Summary of Events and Information	Remarks and references to Appendices
MERTEN Germany.	21.7.19		Parade 08.30 to 08.45. P.T. 09.15-12.15. Parade for line of ROSBERG. 14.15-16.30. Traffic Bridging. One view eastern cofferdam A. sent to RHEINBACH for refectory of magneal Bomb pumping set 07.30 hrs.	
	22.7.19		Parade 08.00-08.45 P.T. 09.15-16.30 work Pontoon equipment & Pontoons on own land.	
	23.7.19		Parade 08.00-08.45 P.T. 09.15-12.15 Swimm. P.m. Recreation.	
	24.7.19		Parade 08.00-08.45 P.T. 09.15-16.30. Authorised Bridging.	
	25.7.19		Parade 08.00-08.45 P.T. 09.15 to 16.30 Knots etc lashing & lazying Coy. siting 2nd Army at 3rd Eagle Sheet to LD. Pier with Beatte	
	26.7.19		Parade 08.00-08.45 P.T. 09.15 to 12.15 Salute & Compliments Swimming. Voluntary Channel Range at 18.30 ROSBERG.	
	27.7.19			
	28.7.19		Parade 08.00 08.45 P.T. 09.15-16.30 Continued Bridging -	
	29.7.19		Parades as 28th	
	30.7.19		08.00-08.45 P.T. 09.15-12.15 Knots etc lashing etc pool out & before lunching inspection. 09.30 two magneal bombs detected in own. Who proceeded to RHEINBACH on 21.7.19.	
	31.7.19		08.00-08.45 P.T. Parade 09.15-16.30 Road Reconnaissance of Bridge equivalent & mining.	
			Cant. E. C. F. JAMES Lewis Compton on Field Engineer. Office IX Corps on Field Engineer.	

(A8804) D. D. & L., London, E.C. Wt. W1771/M231 750,000 5/17 Sch. 52 Forms/C2118/14

Army Form C. 2118.

WAR DIARY
INTELLIGENCE SUMMARY. 76th Field Coy. R.E. Sheet 1.
WESTERN DIVISION.

(Erase heading not required.)

Instructions regarding War Diaries and Intelligence Summaries are contained in F. S. Regs., Part II. and the Staff Manual respectively. Title pages will be prepared in manuscript.

Place	Date	Hour	Summary of Events and Information	Remarks and references to Appendices
MERTEN Germany	1.7.19		No. 1 Section engaged unloading Company Stores, ietc., on waggons etc. No. 2 Section working at EICKHOLZ SCHLOSS on Divnl. O. C. dugout work in Divisional area. No. 3 Section BONN with Bde Pontoon Bridge.	
	2.7.19		No. 2 Section - replace codehouses between incinerators, wash houses etc. in 1st Brigade area.	
	3.7.19		Work as 1st. No. 3 Section return to MERTEN from BONN.	
	4.7.19		Work as 1st. ALFTER to be taken over by Section of 409 Field Coy R.E.	
	5.7.19		Work as 1st. No. 3 Section overhauling R.E. wagons etc. No. 4 Section returns to MERTEN from ALFTER.	
	6.7.19		Work as 1st. No. 4 Section now 409 Field Co. Owing to visit of Sections now 10.40 a.m. Sudan. C.in C. to pause -	
	7.7.19		Company state monthly training. 06.00 to 08.45 Physical Exercises. 07.15 " 10.15 Saluting Drill. Steady Drill. 10.30 " 11.30 Rifle Exercises. 11.45 " 12.15 Musketry care of arms. 12.15 Pamphlet lecture on various subjects. 14.00 hrs parade. Training in morning are 7th. 14.50 hrs to 16.30 hrs (afternoon) was Rifle Exercises + training worked.	
	8.7.19		Physical Trg from 07.30 - 09.15 Parade with Bore Explained, with tests at 09.45. Rifle Exercises at 10.15 Instructional Lecture on Army Reorganization from One Month leave to England after Ziegefield + January.	
	9.7.19			

Army Form C. 2118.

WAR DIARY
INTELLIGENCE SUMMARY
(Erase heading not required.)

76th Field Coy R.E.
WESTERN DIVISION.

Sheet 2.

Place	Date	Hour	Summary of Events and Information	Remarks and references to Appendices
MERTEN Germany	10.7.19		Training carried on. Football contest. Packsaddlery, Packing Equipment.	
	11.7.19		Parade as 7th P.T. Rifle Exercises, Musketry Instruction Squad Drill Open Order, Rifle Exercises, Musketry Knee straining exercise.	
	12.7.19	08-00 to 08-45 P.T. 09.30 Parade of all O.R. to Medical Inspection. victualling. Recreation busy.		
	13.7.19		Church Parade at 10.40 hrs. All denominations except R.C. formed units to service. Offertaking taken for poor.	
	14.7.19		Parade at same hours as 7th M.P.T. Squad Drill with Arms Bayonet Rifle Musketry Position Instruction.	
	15.7.19		Parade as on 7th P.T. Squad Drill extending Rifle Musketry, open training. Recreation met. Stores received Cable Cricket	
	16.7.19		Parade as 7th P.T. Section Drill Extended Order Musketry. Cricket match. Officers v. men's Coy at 14.00.	
	17.7.19		Parade. P.T. as 7th 08-45. 09-15 - 16.30 Trestle Bridging.	
	18.7.19		Parade 05-00 5.30 P.T. 06.30 to 17.30 M.T. Section hostel taken transport waggon at 30 3rd Brigade.	
	19.7.19		General holiday in the celebration of Peace.	
	20.7.19		Sunday. Church Parade. Voluntier at Rostery 15.30.	

Army Form C. 2118.

76th Field Co R.E.
WESTERN DIVISION
Sheet 4

WAR DIARY
or
INTELLIGENCE SUMMARY.
(Erase heading not required.)

Instructions regarding War Diaries and Intelligence Summaries are contained in F.S. Regs., Part II. and the Staff Manual respectively. Title pages will be prepared in manuscript.

Place	Date	Hour	Summary of Events and Information	Remarks and references to Appendices
MERTEN Germany.	31.7.19		Officers with Company. Capt A.T. COLVILLE. Lieut C.J. CREER M.C. " W. REID. M.C. Stores Officer. D.E. 2 Lt. A.C. JENNINGS. " N.A. BLANDFORD NEWSON " E.W.F CRAGGS (in Hospital) July 31st 1919.	A.T. Colville. Major R.E. O.C. 76 Field Co R.E.

CONFIDENTIAL

ORIGINAL

WAR DIARY

of the

76th Field Company
R.E.

for the month of

AUGUST 1919

Army Form C. 2118.

WAR DIARY
INTELLIGENCE SUMMARY.
(Erase heading not required.)

76th Field Company. R.E.
Western Division —

Instructions regarding War Diaries and Intelligence Summaries are contained in F. S. Regs., Part II. and the Staff Manual respectively. Title pages will be prepared in manuscript.

Place	Date	Hour	Summary of Events and Information	Remarks and references to Appendices
MERTEN Germany.	1.8.19.		Parades for drill training. 08.00 to 08.45. P.T. 09.15 – 16.30. Tentoon trestles & pontoon manned.	
	2.8.19.		Tents & pontoons wagons packed all R.E. material collected & put away. Instruction in manning of pontoons. Capt. Calverley entertainment for Blanco and Cpl. Whitehead got placed.	
	3.8.19.		Sunday. Voluntary Church Parade.	
	4.8.19.		Bank holiday. General holiday to all R.E. Men employed on training other reconnaissance for Company Sports.	
	5.8.19.		Company Sports quite successful. Open events for D.E. and Mule draft Mule and tent pegging also Mule racing were thoroughly enjoyed & all items were full of interest to the last.	
	6.8.19.			
	7.8.19.		Parades. 07.00 to 12.15. 14.00 to 16.30. Dismounts & photographs. Cleaning transport. All vehicles etc in Company.	
	8.8.19.		2Lt. N.A. BLANDFORD NEWSON transferred to 93rd Field Coy R.E. with 3 N.C.O's. Company employed on demobilization & preparation for cleaning vehicles etc. 40.7 Active Service Cart was handed over to R.E. Park at cross roads 4 Kms. N. of IX Corps outage also ROMER 40F.	

Army Form C 2118.

WAR DIARY
or
INTELLIGENCE SUMMARY.
(Erase heading not required.)

76th Field Company RE
Western Division

Instructions regarding War Diaries and Intelligence Summaries are contained in F. S. Regs., Part II. and the Staff Manual respectively. Title pages will be prepared in manuscript.

Place	Date	Hour	Summary of Events and Information	Remarks and references to Appendices
MERTEN Germany.	9.8.19.		Parade from 09.00 to 12.15. General work. All vehicles cleaned. Church Parade 19.00.	2
	10.8.19.		Sunday. Voluntary Services at ROSBERG.	
	11.8.19.		Parade as 8th. One section took Lewis and Vickers MG for instructional purposes. Pontoon strata dismantled and checked.	
	12.8.19.		Work as on 11th.	
	13.8.19.		Work as on 11th. Instruction by 3 m.g. schools. Cricket match Marrieds v Singles.	
	14.8.19.		Work as on 11th. Completed photographs in town.	
	15.8.19.		Work & parade as on 11th.	
	16.8.19.		Work as on 11th. Preparing m.t.	
	17.8.19.		Sunday.	
	18.8.19.		Party of Lieut. [?] & detachment sent to BONN in connection with entertaining high rank officers at BONN as well. Three GS waggons & two limbered carts & horses sent to BONN.	
	19.8.19.		Work parade as 11th. Our horses sent to RODENKIRCHEN. Rifles & bayonets handed into Ord. Parties sent to Transport except 60 rounds S.A.A. per man & IX Corps. All m.t. also equipment.	

Army Form C. 2118.

WAR DIARY
or
INTELLIGENCE SUMMARY.
708 Full Coy. R.E.
Western Division

(Erase heading not required.)

Place	Date	Hour	Summary of Events and Information	Remarks and references to Appendices
MERTEN Germany	20.8.19.		All equipment of Company leaves BONN at 15.00 hrs entraining for ANTWERP. 1st Lt. A/C. JENNINGS in charge of RODENKIRCHEN. Riders stand by Coy. huts and parade for use as on 11th Clearing area. Meals etc. Lt CREED handed 14 & 18½ engr U.K. Leave to WEILERSWIST entrainment. Lower passage on 11th Ridge U.K.	
	21.8.19.		Continued DE Count at 19.30 hrs at MERTEN.	
	22.8.19.		All cycles & motor cycles turned in to DADOS, A.S.C. M.T. Coy. Completed turned in to take equipment etc. Passage on 11½ complete cleaning up etc.	
	23.8.19.		Company personnel leaves at 07.90 for March. All at 10.30 hrs Entrain at ROISDORF at 15.00 hrs. Entrained strength 3 officers 158 O.R.	
Troop Train	24.8.19.		Troop train renders journey.	
	25.8.19.		Company detrain at CALAIS at 05.00 and entrain for DOVER enroute to KINMEL PARK CAMP at 10.15 hrs after completion 4 years overseas service on the Western Front.	

Signatures—
Major T. R. Rozne M.C.
Capt A/C. COLVILLE.
F.Lt. E.W.F. CRAGGS.

Lt. C. J. CREED M.C. on leave
F.Lt A/C. JENNINGS with equipment.
Lt. W. REID M.C. DE Stores officer.

KINMEL PARK CAMP.
28.8.19.

C. R. Rozne
Major R.E.
O.C. 708 Field Coy R.E.

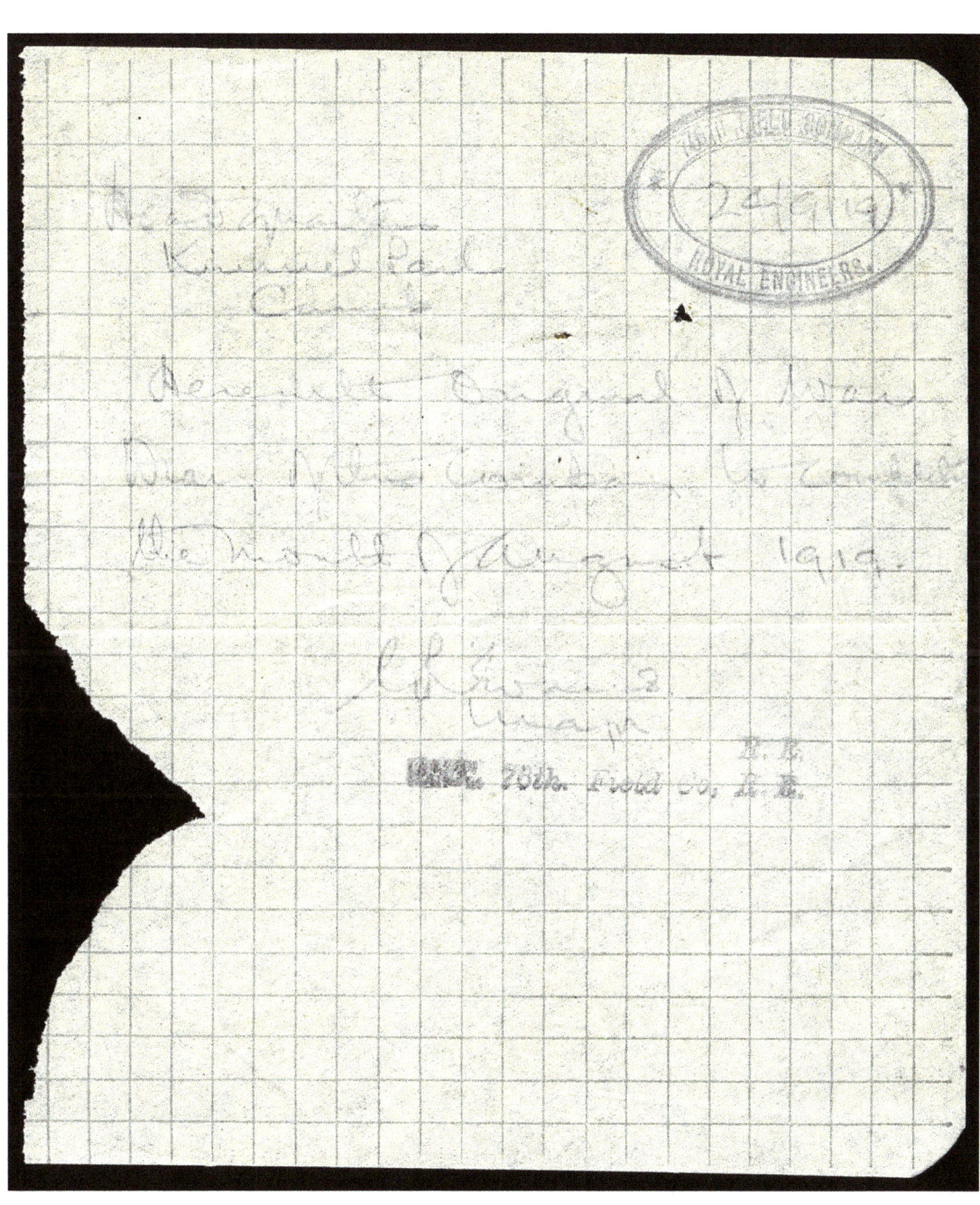

SECRET

ORIGINAL
WAR DIARY of the
76th Field Co. RE.
to complete
the month
of
August 1919

Army Form C.2118.

WAR DIARY
~~or~~
INTELLIGENCE SUMMARY. 76th Field Cy R.E.
Western Division

(Erase heading not required.)

Instructions regarding War Diaries and Intelligence Summaries are contained in F.S. Regs., Part II. and the Staff Manual respectively. Title pages will be prepared in manuscript.

Place	Date	Hour	Summary of Events and Information	Remarks and references to Appendices
Kinmel Park Camp	26.8.19		Company engaged in dismantling Barrack furniture etc. fittings, cutting grass, drawn Rations, wheels, chains up previous accounts - Coy Orders on duties, fatigues etc.	
	27.8.19		do.	
	28.8.19		do. — Revd Reid returns to duty with Company.	
	29.8.19		Fatigues harvest inspection.	
	30.8.19		Parade Services in our demobilisation tent.	
	31.8.19		Officers present with Company:— Capt. A.J. Coleridge Lieut. C.J. Guest M.C. " Jo. Reid M.C. 2/Lt. Ew.T Crozer a.c. Journeys.	

Kinmel Park Camp Sept 1st 1919.

R.Thomas Major R.E.
O.C. 76 Field Cy R.E.

(A7092). Wt. W12830/M1293 75 10/20. 1/17. D.D. & L., Ltd. Forms/C2118/14.

www.ingramcontent.com/pod-product-compliance
Lightning Source LLC
Chambersburg PA
CBHW081502160426

43193CB00014B/2564